BE A POWERFUL LIFE COACH

THE SECRET TO MORE CLIENTS, MORE COACHING, AND MORE WEALTH

DANIEL ROBBINS

INTRODUCTION

If you're a life coach and want to take your business to the next level, or if you're just starting out – allow this book to be your guide. We'll cover topics such as ways to get more Life Coaching Clients in the easiest, fastest, and most profitable way.

Take these steps and with time and perseverance you'll have a thriving practice and be living a rewarding life, filled with financial success as a coach.

My plan is to take you through a process to get a surge of clients in as little as 30 days and implement your coaching skills faster than ever.

ONE

Be an Effective Life Coach

LIFE COACHING IS one of the top earning businesses today. Since everybody aims to be successful and happy, people seek for these professionals to guide them and teach them on how to look at life from a different perspective and address their emotional needs.

For example, a coaching client named Rita was struggling about her image. For years, she'd been stressing herself on losing weight, going to the gym every day, and experimenting with different diets but nothing seemed to work for her. Then one day a life coach named Rob approached her and asked her to attend one coaching session for free, just so she could see if coaching was something she could benefit from.

The woman was pleasantly surprised how the Rob encouraged her and taught her how to view herself and her weight loss challenges from different perspectives that made her feel completely different. Long story short, Rita continued to attend weekly sessions with Rob. She said that she never felt happier and more content with where she was in life.

The main goal of life coaching is to make people's lives happier and more successful. It helps people realize their current mistakes and see them as an opportunity to learn; and it also focuses on what is in the present moment and looking at possibilities for the future, instead of stressing out over mistakes or failures from the past. Some may consider it related to psychology and counseling, although it does not function the same way as these two.

Life coaching is also different from psychoanalysis and psychotherapy. This field does not cure depression or any psychological problems. Rather, it presents options so that they can feel in control of the situation. Coaching presents an opportunity to be more satisfied with their lives, achieve their goals, plan their future and enjoy everything they have (both tangible and intangible).

To be a powerful life coach, you should be effective and successful at the same time. What does that mean?

An effective life coach means that most, if not all, of your clients are satisfied with your work. You should be able to capture their heart and immediately connect with them. You should establish a sense of trust with the client.

Trust is a very important aspect of this relationship because the client will be giving you confidential information about their feelings, goals in life, fears, etc. This is an essential tool so that the life coach can effectively give advice to the client, and more importantly guide the client to finding answers on their own with the use of powerful questions. In the first half of this E-book, you will learn more about the tools in becoming an effective life coach.

On the other hand, to be a successful life coach, you

need to be effective and at the same time, you need to make money. Although this profession is centered on helping others, you should also remember that this is a form of business. Proper marketing strategies should be followed so that you will be able to sell yourself.

If you are a newbie and you are not a part of a coaching institution, it will be more challenging for you to gain clients. In the second half of this E-book, you will learn more about marketing strategies that will take you to the top of your career ladder and help you make more money you can ever imagine.

Being successful and effective should go hand in hand. Without both, you cannot be a powerful life coach. You can't attract clients, you can't make money and you will never be fully satisfied in this profession. Allow this book to be your ultimate guide to success in your life-coaching career.

TWO

The Power of Books and Learning

ARE YOU AN UNDERGRADUATE? Or are you working? Whether you are a student or already an employee, a businessman or a doctorate degree holder, you can be a life coach. The first step is to get courses about life coaching. Whether you decide to get an undergraduate degree or extra courses, it is very important if you are well educated in this field. Not only will this add credibility, but also this can keep you confident in your career – the more you know, the more effective you become.

If you are already a life coach and you are still having doubts about your potential or you still lack confidence, read books. This will give you the power to stand in front of the client and address their concerns and queries without any hesitation or fear. Never forget that there's always room for improvement and one must not stop reading and learning.

Here are some suggestions of programs where you can further enhance your learning:

Coaches Training Institute (CTI)

Liberty University Online

OEDB Online Life Coaching Degrees (Bachelor's and Master's Degrees)Prescott College Certificate in Coaching

GetEducated.com College Degree programs

Howard Community College Professional Coaching Program

PEOPLE MAGNET

One aspect life coaches should remember is the power to attract people. This is the step to gaining more clients and gaining more money. However, one struggle that many life coaches encounter is the lack of confidence. You cannot be a "people magnet" if you are afraid of people. Problems such as fear of rejection, being laughed at, humiliation and, the worst thing, fear of failure will drag a life coach's career to the ground. The following are the quick and easy steps that you can follow to conquer and surpass this fear and have the right mindset for this job.

1. **Embrace the Fear**

The problem is you are afraid of your fear. You should actually embrace it. Face it. Ask it. If you do not have the courage to address this problem, it will forever haunt you.

Whenever you feel that you are afraid of approaching a client or suggesting options, confront this feeling. You'll be amazed at what you can do if you just go out there and confront it. Imagine it as if you are talking to your fear. Admit that you are afraid. Be curious about what is behind the fear. Ask it. Embrace the feeling of being afraid. Stay like this until the fear subsides.

Never escape from your fear; embrace it and let it be your strength. If you are afraid to talk to a client, accept that you are afraid but do not let it hinder your job. Fight it. Embrace it up to the last minute.

In the long run, you will see how important it is to embrace, hold on to, and finally let go of the fear. You may fail sometimes, and that is a good thing because each time you fail, the stronger you become because you can learn from your mistakes and do better next time.

2. **Take risks**

As a life coach, you will be given a variety of scenarios. Some of those might be stressful and may be uncomfortable for you. In this case, never hesitate to take risks. Go out of your comfort zone. After all, that is what you encourage your clients to do, so let's lead by example. In this way, you will be able to improve, learn from your mistakes and advance to the next level. Be strong and do not be afraid to fail because failure is inevitable. The most successful people including Albert Einstein, Steve Jobs, and Richard Branson have all failed. It is one of the main ingredients to success.

3. **A Model to Your Clients**

Since you are the one giving advice to the clients, you cannot deny the fact that they will see you as a role model in their lives. People who are potential clients often show signs of anxiety and lack of confidence and the ability to handle the situation. As a life coach, you should be able to possess the opposite of those traits. This can also build trust and credibility. Let us take this scenario as an example:

Maria stumbled upon two life coaches. They are extremely different from one another. She was able to talk, for a couple of sessions, with both life coaches and here's her summary of their traits.

Life Coach 1: Will

Traits: Not Afraid of Anything, Knowledgeable, Arrogant, Forgets Appointments, Talks a lot without giving the client a chance to share

LIFE COACH 2: **Spencer**

Traits: Knowledgeable, Empathetic, Listener, Diligent, Hard working, Organized, A Motivational Speaker, Clumsy and sometimes Forgetful

MARIA CHOSE to continue her sessions with Spencer because she can see him as a person she wanted to be. Although both coaches are forgetful, Maria sees that she can trust Spencer. The ability to listen and to empathize with the client is one of the essential keys to effective life coaching. So, remember that a good first impression is important and sustaining it is a must. You should show your client that you are credible enough to be hired.

Also keep in mind that people who seek life coaches are generally those who are lost or feel stuck and can't make a clear decision about the direction of their future. Therefore, it is best to either have the naturally skills to be a good listener or learn them.

THREE

Ideal Life Coach

PUT yourself in the shoes of the client. What are traits that you desire in the life coach you want to hire? This "putting yourself in the shoes of others" illustration will give you the idea of what makes an ideal life coach. You are dealing with people so you should be sensitive in everything you say and do. Here's a good strategy on how you could be the ideal life coach. It is divided into 2 parts: the soft area and the hard area.

- Listening to the client's story
- Asking Questions That Get The Clients Curious About Their Life
- Showing you understood their point and situation
- Telling your standpoint

- Explaining your point

- Presenting the options

- Emphasizing your point

Soft Area

As you can see, when listening to the client's story and asking questions, it is important to be empathetic and understanding. You should be an excellent listener. You should be able to put yourself in the shoes of your client. What are his or her feelings? What are the things he or she is thinking?

In this way, you will show that you genuinely care about them. You should make them feel that their emotions are the most important thing in the world and you are willing to address it with all your heart. The soft area is the representation of the situations wherein you need to slow down, be understanding, and empathize with the client.

Hard Area

On the other hand, the hard area is the situations wherein you need to be firm. You have to emphasize your point and be encouraging so that the client will also trust himself or herself in doing the right thing to do. For example, a client is confused on what to prioritize – getting married or advancing on his or her career ladder - the life coach should emphasize the good and bad points of both decisions – which are brought out by asking the client powerful questions.

If the coach has an opinion, he should be clear that it is his opinion or perspective and not the best way, but instead another option that that client can either take or leave – no strings attached. Most importantly, the client knows deep down what is best for him or her. In the end, you should always let the client decide on what to do. You are the agent to guide him or her to realizing what he or she really wanted.

FOUR

Be the Successful Life Coach

YOUR AIM IS NOT JUST to help others but also to gain profit from it; therefore you need marketing strategies to gain an edge over the competition. There are basic marketing strategies you can use on your journey. You can choose what is best for you, your working style and also, your situation. The first half of the book plus these nine marketing strategies will guarantee 30-day success in your life-coaching career. Just be diligent and do not give up on your goal.

THE MAIN CONCEPT of this 30-day success program is that you need to start small. After planting your business in your local network, the next step is to get an alliance or a team than will be your connection to other localities. This diagram will illustrate how this program works.

THE TRICK IS to start small. The "You" is the core to your success. You have to be fully prepared and see yourself succeeding in order to be successful in this journey. First-degree potential clients are the ones located in your community that you already know. These can include friends, family, acquaintances, and colleagues. Second Degree includes potential clients who are friends of friends, and people you are planning on meeting outside of you direct circle of influence - for instance, if you met someone today in the grocery store, or a few new people at a networking event. Third degree includes those you've met through the

Internet and through word of mouth. These include people that have found your website, or people you've met through Facebook, or LinkedIn. All of these are needed, and when you're first starting out it's best to begin with the first degree to build comfort with your skills, and then reach out to the second and third degrees so that it becomes second nature and feels natural to meet new people for coaching.

FIVE

Sample Sessions

THIS IS the easiest of the nine marketing strategies. This is advisable for those who are starting their business as a life coach and those who are working alone. Sample sessions will enable your potential clients to have a sneak peek into your life coaching skills. Most clients like to attend these free sessions so that they can gauge if you pass their standards or not. This is also your chance to show the client your ability to help them solve their problem.

Start small. This is the first step to your journey to success. A good start will definitely boost your business three or four steps ahead. The following are your tips on how you'll make your free sessions worth it.

1. Be prepared. A life coach, just like any other employee, should be on time. Make sure you have done the prepara-

tions written in the first part of this eBook. Make sure you are confident and approachable to gain the client's trust.

2. Keep in mind that "First Impressions Last". As it was said in the first part of the book, do not neglect the power of first impressions. If people already like you on your initial meeting, they will most likely hire you as a life coach and would definitely refer you to their friends.

3. Be concerned, understanding and focused. Make your client feel that you are 100% focused on your session. Your goal is to make her feel comfortable and gain her trust.

4. Be natural, but do not overdo it. Some life coaches tend to be so energetic and overreacting. This behavior might scare the clients. Just be yourself. Talk to the clients with concern and understanding. Smile at them (they can hear a smile on the phone too). Be accommodating.

5. Promote your free sessions through your website, social media accounts, brochures, and business cards so that people will know about it.

SIX

Free Sample Session Rules For Success:

RULE#1: **Each client you give free coaching sessions to - no matter what - ask them if they want to be a client.**

This way you can get practice to be more comfortable and skilled at asking, and of course gain clients from it, eventually leading to the life you want to live.

IN BECOMING A SUCCESSFUL LIFE COACH, you should be effective, and at the same time, you should make money because money is what will lead you to become financially successful.

THIS IS CHALLENGING for many coaches because there is such a high out of coaching and helping others. Although,

I you need to be making enough money to live the life you desire, not only enough money to survive.

TAKE A LOOK AT YOUR COACHING. How many free sample sessions are you giving per week? How many of those convert into paying clients? How many paying clients do you need to sustain your life? How many clients do you want to be living the life you desire?

OFTEN COACHES ARE fearful to ask the coachee to be a paying client, even though he or she was very grateful and thankful for the value you'd just given them. So how much do you want to charge?

SOMETIMES IT TAKES a perspective shift towards money and looking at it from a perspective of value. People want coaching because they want change – they want results – and coaching keeps them on track, keeps challenging them, and doesn't let them slip back into their old habits. That is the value they will give receive – which is extremely valuable. People who are willing to pay and add value to their lives are the people you want to coach. They will be more financially invested and therefore more motivated to change.

RULE #2: Give the "Free Sample Sessions" An Enticing Name And Include 3 Reasons For Why They Would Want It

. . .

REALLY EVERYBODY COULD USE a life coach from time to time, right? However, the problem is most people don't understand the value that a coach can bring into their lives. That is why it is important when offering people free 30-minute sample sessions, to tell them what they will receive so you'll be more likely hear a "Yes, I'd love to" than a "No, thanks". Give each of your "Free Sample Sessions" a snazzy title, such as "Get Unstuck And Feel Alive Again" or "Find Your Perfect Match Today", or "Rediscover Your Passion".

IN ADDITION STRESS the importance of making it sound like the person needs it, and that no matter what the person will receive value from it. Keep in mind that you always want to be honest – don't promise what you can't give just make what you can give sound enticing so the coachee will bite. Include 3 compelling reasons for why someone would want the session you've created. Make them powerful outcomes so that your ideal client would feel like they have to try it out.

RULE #3: Limit The Sessions & Your Availability

It is important to make yourself sound like you are in high demand. Make it sound like the coachee is very fortunate if they get offered a session with you. For example, "This Monday and Wednesday, I am offering 5 Rediscover Your Passion Sessions to the first 5 people who email me @_____. You won't want to miss out!" You can do this once a month (or whatever timeframe works for you) until you have your ideal number of clients.

SEVEN

Website and Social Networking Sites

WHEN YOU ARE STILL STARTING and you do not have enough money to spend on marketing, free websites and social networking sites are the best avenues for promoting your business. Since a good chunk of people are Internet savvy, you can easily reach them through the Internet. Start promoting your site to your friends and ask them to share it to others.

BUILDING **your site**

If you are not knowledgeable about online marketing, you can ask a friend to help you with this, or there are several free websites out there that you can use to easily put up a website. A few of my favorites include:

- www.wordpress.com
- www.weebly.com

HOWEVER, if you have the money to pay for a professional, it's a good investment for your business. Just make sure you have the following in your website:

- Your Name
- A short description about you

(Include the schools you've attended especially the ones related to life coaching, courses you took, and your strengths as a life coach.)

- Business description
- Contact numbers, e-mail, and address

(Especially when you have a business space)

- Online Help

(So that the clients will be able to reach you immediately for queries)

SOCIAL NETWORKING SITES

Make accounts on Twitter, Facebook, and LinkedIn. These are three popular sites you can use to spread the information about your business.

Create a business page on Facebook, seek help from your friends, and ask if they can share it to their friends.

Create an account on Twitter. Follow friends and also other people. Keep on following people so that they'll know about you and your business. And post updates of any promotions you are offering.

TIPS:

1. SEO

Gaining hits on the Internet is very difficult. You need to use search engine optimization (SEO) to rank on the search engines. For example, a client searches "life coach in California". If you do not use SEO, your site will not appear anywhere near the top results. All websites are using this technique to raise their rank in the search engine results. So if you want to increase your website's visibility, hire a professional to create your website. If you do not have a budget, then you can find online tutorials on how to optimize your site. www.youtube.com offers a lot of SEO strategies.

2. Always release fresh content.

Whether it is an article or a short post, make sure it has sense. People love reading about new and fresh ideas. Keep on posting interesting content and you will gain numerous followers and clients.

3. Maintain your Reputation

Never ever post anything that will tarnish your reputation. Watch your words and keep every post on a positive note. Always be friendly and do not show signs of anger or frustration.

. . .

4. Connect with other Life Coaching Institutions

Find pages that are also related to your line of work. This will also build harmonious relationships with other businesses plus you can also access their sets of clients.

LOCALS

SINCE YOU ARE BUILDING your ladder to success, the roots should be planted firmly to the ground. The best way to do this is to secure your clients in your local network. This means, before heading to the national level, start with your neighborhood. Distribute business cards. Tell your friends about your business. Ask them if they know someone who needs the service you are offering. After having these sets of clients, you can take the next step, which is the national level.

Here's a quick guide on gaining local clients.

1. Ask help from your friends.

FIRST THING TO do is to ask your friends if they know someone who needs life coaching. You can also ask them to share your website, like your page on Facebook and follow you on Twitter. In this way, you can already access 2nd degree potential clients, and in the long run, third degree ones.

1. Attend local events.

WHENEVER THE COMMUNITY HAS EVENTS, show up. This is your time to share your business with other people. These events will attract people - which mean more potential clients for you. Good sites to find networking events include: www.meetup.com and www.eventbrite.com.

1. Set up an office in your neighborhood.

ALTHOUGH COACHING over the phone is widely accepted, having an office in the neighborhood will attract local clients because it provides access to those people who need the service right away. Also, some people would want to see for themselves the service rather than check it through the Internet.

1. Post announcements on your community bulletin board.

IF YOUR NEIGHBORHOOD has a community board, posting your advertisement will provide access for those people who are not Internet savvy.

1. Advertise through institutions such as schools, churches, hospitals, etc.

IN YOUR LOCAL COMMUNITY, post on the bulletin boards of hospitals, schools, churches, etc. This will spread the word in your entire community.

1. Give out brochures once in a while.

IF YOU STILL HAVE TIME, distribute brochures so that people will be able to read about you and your business. Also include testimonials of past and existing clients if possible.

1. Business Cards

REMEMBER to make your business cards presentable. You should include your motto as a life coach. Always bring a few before you head out of your house because there's no telling when you will need such cards.

ESTABLISHING a good reputation in your community is a stepping-stone to a wider and broader business. So get out there, and make yourself known!

EIGHT

Testimonials

After you have gained a number of clients, ask them to write testimonials about your performance and the impact it has had on them. This will attract other clients because they will have an idea on what kind of life coach you are.

Testimonials can be included in the social networking sites, your website, and your business cards or even on your brochures. These are the areas wherein you can gain an audience who can easily read those testimonials.

How to Get Good and Compelling Testimonials

Since you are aiming to gain more clients, your testimonials should be attractive and compelling so you have to choose whom to interview and what to ask.

First of all, your customers should be satisfied with your service. In this way, you will have more options on whom to interview.

1. Looking for the right person

If possible, interview clients who are influential people in your community. For example, you were able to work with the mayor. In this way, your readers will be more convinced since the mayor is a credible source compared to an ordinary individual.

1. Emphasize key points that are related to your business.

LOOK for the testimonial that emphasizes the key points related to life coaching. For example, one client praised the relaxing ambiance of your office while the other client said that you are a professional life coach because you are very considerate and understanding. The client also admired your ability to look at the situation from a wider perspective. The second client's testimonial will be very attractive to future clients rather than the first one.

1. Ask the right questions

THE THINGS you need to ask the clients are:

- How was the service?
- How did the service help you address your problems?
- Did it satisfy you?

AFTER YOU HAVE CONDUCTED the interview and finished writing the testimonials, let your chosen clients read the final output and allow them to edit the parts they are not satisfied with. Also, after publishing, tell your clients to check out the site or the magazine, newspaper, or advertisement where you have included their testimonials. Lastly, thank them. This will ensure a good rapport with your clients all throughout your career.

ARTICLES AND BOOKS

One way to introduce yourself and your coaching style and ability is through writing about it. Online articles and eBooks are two major media resources for selling yourself. In this way you can:

1. Introduce your coaching style.
2. Present your values and ideals as a person.
3. Show your strength as a coach.
4. Sell yourself without being too obvious.

Also, if you have a local newspaper or magazine, ask if you can submit an article or an excerpt of your book so that you can advertise your business to the community.

DELIVER MOTIVATIONAL SPEECHES

If you have already rooted your business in your local area, the next step is to spread the word to other neighborhoods and even to other municipalities and states. Look for an opportunity wherein you can deliver a motivational speech. Start small. Even if the event only has less than fifty people, grab that opportunity. These fifty people are all potential clients so do your best. Your goal is to spread the word, gain additional clients, get referred to other people, and to be invited to other events as a motivational speaker. You have to deliver your speech in different states because of different audiences and more clients.

TIPS ON BEING a Phenomenal Motivational Speaker

1. Look for a topic that can be easily understood. It should be concrete. People should be able to apply it to their lives. Also, consider the event when choosing your topic. If it is about career opportunities, try conceptualizing about a topic related to career problems or career decision-making.

2. **Deliver your speech with confidence.** The moment you enter the event hall, do not show signs of nervousness. Stand tall, smile, and be natural. As you approach the podium, look at the people around you and be friendly. When delivering your speech, emphasize your points well.

3. **Watch your pronunciation and do not stutter.** Your goal is to gain clients so you need to make a good first impression. Practice your speech at home. As much as possible, it should be flawless.

4. **Mention that you are offering your service as a life coach.** Tell your audience that you are offering free initial sessions. This is the best way to attract them to be interested in your service.

5. **At the end of your speech, make sure you mention ways on how to contact you** (e.g. phone number, website, social networking site accounts, and email). You can also give business cards at the end of the event. Tell your audience that you can be approached after the event for further queries and clarifications.

IF YOU WANT to quickly boost your public speaking skills, I highly recommend The Storytelling Method by Matt Morris, where it discusses strategies to be more confident and have fun while public speaking and talking to "strangers".

NINE

Offer Partnership

Once you already have a stable business in your local network and you are planning to expand your business to other states, areas or even countries, you need a partner life coach or a group to help you with it. This could be anyone, a friend who is also a life coach or a classmate from college. Just make sure you share the same sentiments about work and you have similar ideals about life coaching.

How to Maintain Good Partnerships with your Colleagues

1. Treat your Colleagues as Equals

Since you are now working as a team under the same business, you should be considerate of what your colleague/s is/are thinking. One way of doing so is through getting everyone's opinion in decision-making. After that, make a SWOT (strengths, weaknesses, opportunities, threats) analysis on the decisions suggested, and then decide as a group.

1. **Be Respectful**

LEARN HOW TO RESPECT YOUR COLLEAGUES' space and personal lives. Be considerate at all times.

1. **Manage your Emotions**

IF YOU EVER GET ANGRY with one of your colleagues, do not let it show in front of the whole team. Calm down and analyze the situation first. Find time to tell the other person your feelings in a private conversation and settle it in this manner.

1. **Always Communicate**

1. **Be a Good Listener**

1. **Relax and Enjoy the Company of your Colleagues**

SOMETIMES, you should hang out with your colleagues.

Have a night out or dinner once in a while so that you will get to know each other. It will also improve your working relationship.

TEN

Referrals

This could be achieved when you already have a lot of satisfied clients. This is actually the greatest achievement you'll get in marketing your business. This means people like the way you work and are impressed with your performance. If your clients keep on referring you to their friends, this means they are satisfied. This will also mean that you will gain more and more clients in the long run. Just keep your performance up and the clients will keep on coming.

ADVERTISEMENTS

If you already have the budget for funding advertisements, especially online, this can be a good investment. First of all, since you are paying for these advertisements, your page will be visible among the top results in the search engines. Especially on Google, pages that are paid appear first.

. . .

HOW TO MAKE a Good Advertisement for Life Coaching

1. Free Advertisements versus Paid Ads

There are a lot of free advertisements available in the Internet but if you are willing to invest on the paid ones, go for it. This is a good investment for those who are serious about getting huge numbers of clients. Try Google Ads; this will guarantee numerous hits in the search engine results.

1. Promote Yourself by Producing Good Content

AFTER CLICKING the link to your website, the potential client should get the most out of your website. One way is through producing good content. In this way, the client will learn a lot about your service and how you work. Be concise and get straight to the point.

1. Include Testimonials from your Clients

TESTIMONIALS ARE eye candy for your potential clients. This will ensure them that previous clients are satisfied with your work. Review Chapter 7 particularly how to make your testimonials compelling and attractive to your target audience.

ELEVEN

30-Day Success Program

To have a quick recap about the contents of this book, here's a short summary of the program.

1st Step: The Preparation

Keep yourself educated. Read a lot of books and continuously attend seminars so that you will gain confidence for your career.

Fight your fear. Do not be afraid to talk to your clients. The more you think about it, the more you'll attract it. Embrace your fear, accept it, and you will eventually conquer it. You will be stronger than ever.

Remember that as a life coach, you serve as a model to your clients and to other people. Be at your best at all times. Be punctual. Be polite. Be understanding and empathetic. Learn when to be hard on your clients and when to soften up. To learn more about the soft and hard areas, return to chapter 3.

2nd Step: The Action

There are nine marketing strategies to help you on your journey.

1. Free Sessions
2. Websites and Social Networking Sites
3. Locals
4. Testimonials
5. Articles and Books
6. Deliver Motivational Speeches
7. Offer Partnership
8. Referrals
9. Advertisements

AFTERWORD

Being a life coach is often challenging because you have to balance work and emotions. Sometimes you empathize with your clients but you should not be carried away by your emotions. You have to be firm and strong to be able to do your job as a life coach.

You may experience struggle during the first days of your business, but as you continue to follow the program discussed in this book, you'll get the hang of it and you'll be surprised by the results. The key to success is to keep on working; do not stop, even for a day. Be diligent in doing the suggested techniques and strategies. You will eventually reach the top of your career ladder and gain more money.

This 30-day program will guarantee you success on your life-coaching career. Remember to start small; start with preparing yourself on your journey. If you have already gained enough knowledge about life coaching, then you can advance to the second stage, which is marketing. Start with your neighborhood then slowly climb the ladder by reaching the second, third, and nth degree potential clients.

www.ingramcontent.com/pod-product-compliance
Lightning Source LLC
Chambersburg PA
CBHW070037040426
42333CB00040B/1704